MISSION HEROES ARTHUR MARGÖSCHIS

RIGHT REV. A. A. WILLIAMS | D.D. |

MISSION HEROES

ARTHUR MARGÖSCHIS

MISSIONARY AT NAZARETH- 1877-1908.

A BRIEF MENOIR OF HIS LIFE AND LABOURS

"Spent in the Service."

BY THE

RIGHT REV. A. A. WILLIAMS, D.D.,

BISHOP OF TINNEVELLY AND MADURA.

1908.

Contents

Foreword *vii*

Preface *ix*

1. Arthur MargÖschis-a Memoir 1

Foreword

Published by:
TINNEVELLY CHRISTIAN HISTORICAL SOCIETY
2.2.3(4), North Street,
Bungalow Surandai-627859
Tenkasi district (Tirunelveli)
04633-290401, +91 91767 80001,+91 75388 12218
https://christianhistoricalsociety.in
https://tchsportal.co.in/
Email : christianhistorical@gmail.com

MISSION HEROES ARTHUR MARGÖSCHIS
(MISSIONARY AT NAZARETH- 1877-1908.)
in English

BY THE **RIGHT REV. A. A. WILLIAMS, D.D., (BISHOP OF TINNEVELLY AND MADURA.)**

Printed at : TCHS Press

Preface

NOTE.

This brief memoir doc not profess to give a complete account of the life of Arthur Margöschis; but only a few facts in connection with his earlier history and later career. It is loped these will be interesting to those who knew and loved him; and that the record of his devotedness to his Master's cause will arouse and stimulate fresh zeal for the cause he had so near at heart, and for which he gave his life.

The following words of his, in reply to an address of congratulation from Christians and non-Christians, presented to him at Nazareth on the completion of 32 years of mission service, will reveal the true character of the man and the secret of his spiritual strength:

"During all these years I have always felt that the Spirit of God is hovering over us, is always blessing us, and is ever guiding us. When I look back upon the past, I cannot but say that God has all along been bestowing His Eternal love upon me. In all our efforts we must feel the great love of God. The first sermon I preached after my ordination, according to the request of my beloved father was on Psa. cxvi. 13, 'What shall I render unto the Lord for all His benefits toward me? I will take the cup of salvation, and call upon the Name of the Lord.' Its subject matter has been the key-note of my life. I have at heart the welfare of my flock including good sheep and bad sheep, for all are mine. Visitors come, and they speak of the work carried on here, but for my part I see nothing wonderful. You offer me your congratulations for the efforts I have made for your good. It is true that my career has been a long one, and it has always been my wish to be useful as far as possible to all classes and creeds, but still I am aware of many short-comings, and in looking back on my life I find ample grounds for thanking my friends for the kindness and the loving feelings, they have always manifested toward me. I offer you all my cordial and grateful thanks, and I hope that the kind feelings which have hitherto existed between you and myself will continue as long as it may please God to give me life and strength to direct, and to co-operate in, all the good work that may be undertaken for the well-being of the people committed to my charge."

CHAPTER ONE

ARTHUR MARGÖSCHIS-A MEMOIR

ARTHUR MARGÖSCHIS-A MEMOIR

DEEP shadow of gloom has recently been cast over Tinnevelly by the death of this veteran Missionary and indefatigable worker. To measure the extent of the loss sustained it is necessary to form some idea of the work accomplished by his single-handed and single-hearted efforts during the long period of 31 years. All his ministerial service was spent in Tinnevelly, and the Christian village of Nazareth will long stand an enduring monument of his earnest zeal and devotion. From early years his mind seemed to be forming itself towards the ideal of service and sacrifice which were the distinguishing characteristics of his later life. He was born of God-fearing parents, at Leamington, on December 24th, 1852, the youngest of a family of eight children. When eleven years of age he was sent to the Grammar School of Maltram - in - Longdendale, Cheshire, and afterwards he went to a similar school at Cowley, near Oxford, where he was distinguished for his knowledge of Scripture. When seventeen he entered the Mission College of Warminster, and when there formed a friendship with a young Italian, who afterwards went with him to St. Augustine's, Canterbury, and is now the Rev. Canon Josa, of British Guiana,

After finishing his course at St. Augustine's he went to London for a time, and entered as a medical student at St. George's Hospital, and subsequently appeared at what was known as the Primary Examination in Anatomy and Physiology at the Royal College of Surgeons. It was at this time that the call to the Mission Field came to him, and he went out to India without appearing for the second, or qualifying, examination for the diploma of M.R.C.S. and L.R.C.P. He had, however, made the most of his opportunity, and had gained a considerable knowledge of medicine and surgery, which enabled him to carry on the work in the dispensary and hospital at Nazareth in a thoroughly efficient manner. One of his intimate friends, a medical man himself, says, "I spent a week with him at Nazareth and witnessed his medical work, and I was astonished to see how facile he was in prescribing and in the performance of surgical operations, some of which were of some magnitude. He was a diligent student of medical literature, and kept himself abreast of the times in spite of his numerous and varied occupations and his delicate state of health, Natives crowded to his hospital. ... He was a wonderful man in every respect; and withal so modest, unassuming, and self-sacrificing; but besides the natives, for whose benefit he laid himself out principally, his services as a medical man were sought by Europeans and officials in the district of Tinnevelly,"

He arrived in Madras 26th October, 1875, not quite old enough for Ordination, and was sent to Dr. Caldwell, afterwards Bishop at Idaiyangudi to study Tamil and acquire some experience in mission work. In 1877 he was ordained Deacon in St. George's Cathedral, Madras, and was Gospeller; he was then appointed assistant missionary at Nazareth, the place where he was destined to spend his whole ministerial life of over thirty years. His first charge at Nazareth was the hospital and schools; for some time he acted as organist and choirmaster as well as pastor. He was advanced to the Priesthood in 1880, when he was appointed missionary in full charge of all the work, and by his unwearied zeal and devotion he made Nazareth a household word in missionary records for its numerous and varied activities. All this is the more remarkable when it is considered that his health was never strong, that he was a suffered from chronic asthma, and that he could get but little sleep in consequence; in spite, however, of his frail body and great physical weakness, his energy was marvelous. The following extracts from his diary, when between seventeen and eighteen years of age, show his intense yearning for a life of useful service for others "Unwell. I trust God will spare me to proclaim His Name and give me power among men." Again: "Not at all well. I pray the Lord to build me up, that He may not call me hence before I have done something to promote His glory among the heathen. Precious Jesus, pray for me." Again: January 1st, 1871—"The Lord in His mercy has spared me to live eighteen years. I would commence the New Year with fresh resolutions, and dedicate myself anew to God. By His help I will try, even now, to work for the good of others. Without doubt, in sparing me thus long, God has something for me to do, even though the time be limited. It may be that I am not long for this world. O Father, prepare me, if it be so, that I may be glad to go Home' and be with Christ, which truly would be far better. I feel that I want humility and earnest love towards

od. I will pray for these, and He will answer." These extracts speak for themselves, and show the intense spirituality of his mind, and his simple trust in God's directing care.

How dear Nazareth was to him I his whole life was wrapped up in it; all the wealth of his devotion and energy lavished upon it. Honoured and loved by all his flock, ever ready to minister to their sorrows, to help them in their difficulties, to compose their differences, to arrange their worldly affairs, to advise them in business transactions, their champion when he thought they were unjustly or harshly treated - No wonder that he gained a warm place in their hearts, and that his name and striking personality penetrated far beyond the limits of his charge, and in addition, that he was regarded as a true friend by his Hindu neighbours. He gained their respect by his extreme fairness and candour, they trusted him, resorted to him in their troubles, consulted him in business matters, because they knew his heart was full of sympathy and his best services were at their disposal. No one, whether Christian or non Christian appealed to him in vain.

*I am indebted to Mr. J. T. Margoschis, of Kenilworth, for these interesting details of bis brother's early life.

To anyone who has visited Nazareth, and seen the work there, it must have seemed nothing less than marvelous, that all the complex machinery of the mission should be controlled and directed by one hand. It was a master-mind that devised and carried into effect the different agencies now in full and efficient operation. It was his delight to see these different efforts for good grow and spread into vigorous life. Fearless and determined, he was not daunted by difficulties; unsparing of himself, he expected those associated with him in the work to give their best for its furtherance. Ever ready to encourage and commend where praise was due, he was no less accustomed to rebuke where he saw slackness or indifference. He tried in all things to be absolutely fair. Impatient of sham or pretence, he was quick to recognize honest work, and to reward merit. Large-hearted and tolerant, he was always ready to see and acknowledge good in those from whom in various ways he differed. And many of his warmest admirers were those who were unable to agree with him in some of the views which he held on religious and social subjects. Animated by strong human instincts, he had a warm welcome for his numerous friends, who made the mission house a house of call, and many bright memories will abide of the happy days spent under his roof, and of the ready hospitality dispensed with open hand and heart; his hearty greeting, his transparent pleasure, his cheery laugh, his quick repartee, never unkind, his unfailing courtesy, his anxiety for the comfort and entertainment of his guests, all tended to make such visits seasons of real enjoyment not soon to be forgotten.

The work which he was enabled to perform at Nazareth was truly a notable one; his powers of organization and administration were of no ordinary kind and degree. A visit to Nazareth was an object-lesson in mission work. Sitting in the mission bungalow, one could see signs of life on all sides, and the hum of the many voices in the various schools fell with pleasant effect upon the ear, as day by day the work went on with unfailing regularity and precision. The church in the centre of the village, with its daily services, to which the people went as a matter of course, gave the tone and spirit to all the activities that were carried on. The village is twenty-three miles distant from Palamcottah, the nearest large town, to which it is hoped it may soon be united by railway communication. It is surrounded on all sides by a teeming heathen population, and well merits the description of an oasis in the desert, bright and fruitful with the results of Christian teaching and influence, amid the prevailing darkness and superstition around. Here one could see schools for all classes: a high school for girls with III pupils; lower secondary and primary for boys and girls; an art industrial school, opened by the Most Reverend the Metropolitan of India (Bishop Johnson) in ISS7, with its 270 pupils, learning eight handicrafts, including, carpentry, black smithy work, tailoring, weaving, embroidering, lace-making, and drawing; two training schools; two orphanages; the Bishop's theological class for training catechists; the Hospital of St. Luke, with an average yearly total of 15,000 new patients of all castes and creeds; a children's mission with its own missioner, supported entirely by the people; a night school for boys who are employed all day, organized by Rev. C. W. Weston, who, since coming to India two years ago, has been placed at Nazareth to learn the work; preaching bands who - itinerate in the surrounding villages. That the work done is effectual, may be judged from the fact that from the upper secondary training school for men, 253 teachers have gone out since its location in Nazareth seven years ago, and from the girls' training school, 312, and these are employed in all parts of the Madras Presidency and in other distant places. Thirty-three girls have passed the matriculation examination of the Madras University from St. John's High School for girls. Several of the young men from Nazareth have enlisted in the army, and are now serving their King, thus testifying to the spirit of loyalty to the Throne, which is one of the marked characteristics of our Indian Christians. One very useful organization is the provident fund, Inaugurated in honour of the Golden Jubilee of Her Majesty the Queen, Empress of India, which provides a substantial bonus to the nominees of a deceased member, and another is a widows' fund, which gives pensions to 62 widows. In the matter of church building the people are displaying much laudable earnestness: in 1997 four new churches were dedicated, and five are now in course of construction.

In addition to the work at Nazareth, the districts of Mudalur and Christianagram were under his charge-manifestly a burden too great for one man, when we consider that the entire burden involved the oversight of 86 congregations, with 11,432 baptized Christians, 704 catechumens under instruction, and 4.372 communicants, with 50 schools containing 2,483 children, all being ministered to by twelve clergymen, and 120 catechists and teachers. The annual income of these combined districts was Rs.10,860 for 1907, or an average of over 14 annas for each man, woman and child in the congregations. Considering that the large majority of our Indian Christians are very poor, this fact is very encouraging those who have no money to give, bring their offering of rice every Sunday, which is presented in God's House during Divine Service,

But the stress of all this accumulated responsibility was bound to tell upon the health and strength of one never very robust, and who has been heard to remark, he never knew what a day's good health was, or a night's good rest-his sleep rarely exceeded three hours, if it reached five it was something quite exceptional. For the last few years signs of breaking up have been painfully apparent, and in 1906 he was obliged to take a trip to Australia from which he derived much benefit. The sea-air always seemed to revive bio; he never could endure the cold air of the hills, and it surely is a record for an Indian cancer of nearly thirty-three years, that he never once went to a hill station for a change

His worth and work were recognized far beyond the limits of his sphere of duty. He received the thanks of the Madras Government for the work he did in the great famine of 1877, in the supervision and medical care of a famine camp.

In 19or he was one of the two in the Madras Presidency who received the Kaiser-i-Hind medal from the Viceroy, on its first institution.

He had already been appointed a Fellow of the Madras University in 1894, in token of his powers and success as an educationalist, and on the first establishment of the College of Canons by the Bishop of Madras in 1902, he was appointed a Canon of St. George's Cathedral, Madras. But higher than all earthly distinctions he valued the secure hold which he had obtained in the hearts of his people; to minister to their spiritual welfare was his highest joy, nor did he forget their material prosperity. When opportunity occurred he was on the alert to advance the public interests of the place; and many improvements connected with the buildings, the roads, postal and telegraph communication, and other public objects, are due to the untiring vigilance and constant desire that Nazareth should keep in the van of progress material as well as spiritual ; he loved the place and was proud to see it go forward.

His long experience and intimate knowledge of India and its people made his advice much sought after by missionaries and others interested in the cause; his relations with his Bishop were most cordial and his co-operation most helpful. Holding decided views on Church doctrine and order, he never unnecessarily obtruded his opinions upon others, but endeavoured to work loyally and wholeheartedly with all who were seeking to serve the same Master in sincerity and truth. He had the pen of a ready writer, and had a most voluminous correspondence, while his contributions to the public press were numerous and varied.

The end came somewhat unexpectedly. feeling the heat this year more severely than usual, he determined to go to Colombo for a change, and had made all arrangements for his journey. He arrived in Palamcottah about five o'clock on Thursday morning, April 23rd, apparently much fatigued after his long night journey in a bullock coach from Nazareth; having rested at Bishop stowe till the afternoon, he went on to Tuticorin accompanied by Mr. Weston, who was unwcaried in his care and thought for him. As he seemed to be in a very weak state, the doctor who was called in to attend him, urged his remaining in Tuticorin till he should regain his strength for the passage across to Ceylon; accordingly he remained over the following Sunday in the mission house, and on the Sunday evening seemed to be stronger and brighter when retiring to bed. On the Monday morning his servant went in to him early, as usual, and brought him his chota hazri, of which he partook; he then dropped into a quiet sleep, and was left undisturbed for some time; his servant, however, finding that he did not awake, became alarmed, and about eleven o'clock came and informed Mr. Weston, and on going again into his room, it was found that the end had come, and that he had passed away peacefully and painlessly in his sleep. The long life of faithful service and self-sacrificing devotion was ended; the active brain was at rest; "the finger of God touched him and he slept"; he passed away as he had told his friend, Mr. Godden, he expected to do, in his sleep; le died as he himself would have wished, in harness, and entered into his rest, all the sweeter to him aster the burden and heat of the day, borne often amid sharp pain and suffering. "So He giveth His beloved sleep."

It was, of course, felt that Nazareth, the scenes of his earthly labour was the most fitting spot to be his last resting-place; all necessary arrangements for the removal of the body were made by Mr. Weston, upon whom the strain of the last few days had told heavily. He was aided in his labour of love by a few friends in Tuticorin, and the same evening the remains, accompanied to the station by some of the clergy and many native Christians, the church bells the meanwhile tolling, were taken by train to Tinnevelly Bridge, and arrived there between eleven and twelve o'clock at night The news of his death had been dispatched to Palamcottah previously, and the Rev. S. G, Maduram, the pastor in charge, and a large number of his congregation, with some members of the choir, came down to the station and received the body with all reverent solemnity. Borne by six Indian Christians, it was carried from the train and placed on a carriage, and the long procession began its march of over one and a half miles to Holy Trinity Tamil Church, where a special service was held. It was a weird and touching sight to witness the procession as it moved slowly along in the dead of the night, preceded by torch-lights, and to hear the many voices joining in the Christian lyrics which spoke of Christian hope and faith. From the tower of the church sounded the deep tones of the passing bell, and inside a large congregation had assembled to join in the solemn service. A portion of the burial service was read by Mr. Maduram with much feeling. It was about one o'clock when the remains were brought out and again placed on the funeral carriage, and the long journey of twenty-three miles to Nazareth was begun.

It was nearly seven o'clock in the morning before the destination was reached; in the mean. Time great crowds had filled the streets and were awaiting the arrival of the mournful procession. Amid visible signs of genuine grief, it passed through the main street of the village; it was painful to see the sorrow of his people, as they began to realize that their master had been taken from their head, and would be with them no more. The body was placed in the chancel of the church, where it rested till the afternoon. The Rev. E. Joseph made all the necessary arrangements for the funeral, for the long vigil of grief and anxiety had severely told upon Mr. Weston, and he was obliged to take some much needed rest. The Rev. A. J. Godden was out in the district when he received news of the sad event, but he hurried in with all dispatch and reached Nazareth about noon, and helped in arranging the details of the service. It was decided to have the interment at four o'clock p.m., by which time a large number of clergy had come in from the district, and an immense concourse of people overflowed the church. The first full of the service was in Tamil and an address was given by the Rev. D. Perianayagam, the senior priest of Nazareth; the Rev. P. J. Harris, C.M.S., was present and also took part in the service), the second half at the grave in English; the well-known hymns, "For all the saints who from their labors rest" and "Jesus lives," were sung with great solemnity by those present. All present were visibly affected; many were unable to restrain the outward expression of their grief as he was borne peacefully to his Rest on the shoulders of the clergy of the Nazareth Mission, with words of Christian faith and hope. The Collects were taken by the Rev. C. W. Weston, his trusted colleague, and the prayer of committal and the blessing were said by the Rev. A. J. Godden, his old and valued friend of many years. He sleeps in the quiet little English cemetery under the very shadow of his church, not far from the last resting-place of the Rev. T. Brotherton, a former missionary, and of Mrs. Cammerer, the wise of one of the early missionaries in Nazareth.

And now the Church in Tinnevelly mourns the loss of one of its leaders, whose place it is impossible to fill at present. It is only three months ago, that another valued superintending missionary was taken the Rev. A. A. Dignum, a man of great experience who was labouring most earnestly and faithfully in Tuticorin. We pray that God will put it into the hearts of some of those interested in mission work, to offer them for service in this part of the vineyard, and so to carry on the labors of these devoted men. The need is urgent; the cry never sounded out more clearly and pathetically, "Come over and help us"; may it reach some hearts, and stir up some souls to offer themselves, and fill up the gaps in the ranks of the Soldiers of the Cross in Tinnevelly!

The day following the funeral a meeting of parishioners was held, at which it was unanimously decided to raise a memorial to perpetuate his life and labours in Nazareth, and it was resolved to take steps to erect a new church to replace the existing one. The present building, though enlarged by Canon Margöschis, is quite inadequate to the wants of the mission, and it was a wish very dear to his heart, to replace it by a more worthy and commodious structure,Tablets will also be created to his memory. A committee was formed, and it is confidently hoped that all his many friends, and all who have known, or heard of his unique and remarkable labours, will give their sympathy and assistance to enable the committee to carry out this cherished desire of his life, The Bishop was nominated president of the committee; the Rey, C. W. Weston, Nazareth, secretary; and the Rev. G. H. Smith, secretary, S.P.G., Madras, treasurer; and they will be glad to furnish any information on the subject.

Another scheme which cost him considerable anxiety, and in which he was actively employed Up to his death, was the creation of new buildings for St. John's High School for Girls, Nazareth. The present class-rooms are quite unworthy, and some of them in almost an unsafe condition, most of the necessary funds for this purpose have been promised, The S.P.G. have voted £1000 from the Marriott Bequest, the S.P.C.K. 4250, and the people of Nazareth themselves have promised Rs. 1000. Canon Brittain, late acting Archdeacon of Madras, who has always taken a warm interest in Nazareth, also very kindly associated himself with the scheme, and has raised about Rs.1500 for its furtherance; for his sympathy and efforts in this direction we are deeply grateful; also for an additional sum of about Rs.1500, which he collected to make good the loss of Rs.14,000 sustained by the Mission in the disastrous failure of Arbuthnot & Co., Madras, in 1906. It is hoped, therefore, that when the consent of Government is obtained, and with its assistance, the erection of the new High School will be proceeded with

It will readily be acknowledged that Canon Margöschis was a man of singular gifts, of strong resolution, of remarkable administrative ability; but these, however notable, did not constitute the real secret of his influence and success. He was al man who lived close to God, a man of great spirituality of life and humility of character sustained through all his days of weakness and pain, by the presence of God. His fellow-laborer who was associated with him in work, and tended him through his illness, writes, "Needless to say I miss him much ; I have learned to love him for his goodness of heart, his kindness and thoughtfulness for others; to esteem him for his many admirable qualities and reverence him for his self-devotion and love to his Master's cause. We thank God for His servant's life and labors; we praise Him for the loan that was lent to us; and we believe God will carry on His work, though He buries His workmen. He has called our brother to the higher service above; he has now entered within the vail, and rests from the labours of earth; but his works do follow 117, and his example will serve as an inspiration to many a toiler as he seeks to carry forward the torch of Divine truth, and to proclaim the Saviors' love for sinners, in some of the dark places of the earth.

"THEY THAT TURN MANY TO RIGHTEOUSNESS
SHALL SHINE AS THE STARS
FOR EVER AND EVER."

THIE END.

9 798888 151686

Printed by Libri Plureos GmbH in Hamburg,
Germany